Rainy Day Games

Projects, Programs, and Play for Rainy Days

by Michelle Decker

American Camping Association®

American Camping Association, Inc.
5000 State Road 67 North
Martinsville, Indiana 46151-7902
765-342-8456 American Camping Association National Office
800-428-CAMP American Camping Association Bookstore
www.ACAcamps.org

     Library of Congress Cataloging-in-Publication Data
Decker, Michelle, 1976-
   Rainy day games: projects, programs, and play for rainy days/Michelle Decker.
    p.cm
   ISBN 0-87603-170-X
   1. Indoor games.   2. Group games.   3. Youth — Recreation.   I. Title.
   GV1229.D43 2001
   790.1'5 — dc21

                                        2001018824

Chapter One

Small Group Activities (10 – 25 campers)

Cabin Fun

Big Spaces Needed

Outdoor Play for Mild Rainy Days

Inside Out Projects

Chapter Two

Chapter 3

All-Camp Activities/All Ages

Cabin Fun

Big Spaces Needed

Outdoor Play for Mild Rainy Days

Inside Out Projects

Additional Resources

Acknowledgments

Several people offered creative insights for this book by brainstorming new activities and reminiscing about fun rainy day activities they did at camp. I would like to thank Kim Barcelona, Andy Decker, Gary Eavey, Anna Gilmore, Ricardo Moraes, Beta Moraes, Rachel Osband, and Carol Stone for their help with this project. I also want to thank Indiana University's Bradford Woods Environmental Education program, which taught me many of the activities included within this book.

Introduction

Camp is filled with laughs and smiles and wonderful experiences that enrich the lives of children each day. It is important that we continue to make that impact on children each day no matter what the weather. Unfortunately, many camp staff face adversity the minute they see those first few raindrops begin to fall. In the changing world of camp, this doesn't have to be the case. With a little bit of preparation before the start of camp and some creative energy, every child will be able to embrace a rainy day and find that soggy shoes are not the end of the world!

Some initial preparation will allow staff to make quick changes without hesitation. Provide staff members with a package of arts and crafts supplies (e.g., construction paper, scissors, markers, crayons, tape, and glue) to use with their group. By placing these items in a dry, safe place for use on rainy days or other special times, staff will find that they are not fighting with other groups over the last set of markers or scissors in the arts and crafts shelter. These will also give some basic starter items for many possible projects. These items should be replenished after their usage, no one wants to find their supplies diminished on the day it is really needed. Along with these supplies, it is nice to tuck away a few ideas from this book or a similar book.

It is also helpful to be prepared with a few quick games that don't require equipment. Games are great for filling time until thoughts can be pulled together and any additional supplies can be gathered. Save a few special games just for rainy days. The campers will find them new and exciting. Be prepared to try new things and to keep smiling and laughing even if something fails or it rains for the third day in a row!

The activities within this book are arranged into three distinct categories/chapters by group size appropriate for the activities; for example, small group activities (10-25 campers); large groups/combination of two or more small groups (25-40+ campers); and all camp activities. Within each chapter, the activities are further subdivided into recommended recreational space. Activities will be listed in three sections: Cabin Fun – appropriate projects and activities to be held in a cabin or between cabins; Big Spaces Needed – activities suitable for large, indoor recreational facilities; Outdoor Play for Mild Rainy Days – features a listing of games for the outdoors; Inside Out Projects – lists activities that can transition from an indoor setting to an outdoor setting once inclement weather subsides. Each activity listing includes the recommended ages, equipment, preparation time, activity description, and possible variations. You should find activities that remind you of old favorites, others that are brand new, and still others that have some unique variations. Overall, this book makes soggy shoes not seem so bad and turns a little bit of rain into a lot more fun!

Safety

Safety first, last, and always is every camp's motto! Rainy days bring on new risks and hazards that need to managed appropriately. Refer to your camp's safety protocols and always use common sense. In addition, the following are safety tips to keep in mind when it begins to get wet outside.

- Take proper cover/shelter or stay inside when it is thundering and lightening! Your camp should have guidelines for dealing with thunderstorms.

- All surfaces become slicker when wet, including grass, mud, pavement, and wood. Do not run on wet surfaces; it is very easy to turn an ankle or fall.

- Remember that wet surfaces outside often lead to wet surfaces inside. Be sure to designate a place to leave wet articles of clothing when coming in and to mop or dry indoor surfaces often. For individual cabins, it may be best to leave all shoes at the door or in screened-in porches. For large gatherings determine a place to leave raincoats and be prepared to mop surfaces afterwards. Always remind campers to slow down because surfaces are wetter than normal.

- No running on damp or wet surfaces.

- Remind campers to wear rain gear to prevent wet clothing. Encourage campers to change into dry clothing whenever possible so they don't get chilled.

- Keep a few extra raincoats around.

- Many animals, such as frogs and salamanders, will be out enjoying the rain. Be cautious of not stepping on them or their homes.

Chapter One

Small Group

(10 – 25 campers)

Cabin Fun

Mars Landing

Ages:

6- to 8-year-olds

Equipment:

Large tarps	Paper
Blankets	Marker and crayons
Chairs	Scissors
Tent poles	Tape

Streamers (not crepe paper, which fades when damp and ruins clothing)

Prep Time:

5 minutes

Activity:

Let's take a ride into the unknown, outer space! But before traveling can begin, a spaceship has to be built. With some help from the counselors, campers can build a spaceship using the supplies listed above and anything else that is around the cabin. Make sure it is built big enough for the whole group to sit under. The spaceship can be decorated with paper and streamers so that it is unique to each cabin group. Once the spaceship is constructed, everyone can sit underneath and decide where to go first. If the counselor stays outside the spaceship, he or she can work the lights, make sound effects, safely "shake" the spaceship, and upon arrival, can become the token alien every good planet needs.

Once campers have landed on the new planet, they can explore all areas of their imaginative destination. For example, strange species with eight long legs and hairy bodies may be lurking in corners, or a new type of edible plant that is red, gummy, and shaped like a teddy bear may be the planet's vegetation. Or, a strange alien speaking a different language may be waiting to greet the group of explorers.

If desired, arrange a visit to the camp director or to the nature center. Just remember to be creative with each new planet that is visited.

Variations:

- Make a time machine instead.
- Go outside the galaxy and make up new planet names.
- Have some of the campers become aliens.
- Design the perfect alien costume.
- Plan a visit to a neighboring planet (another cabin) that has also built a space ship.

Sock Puppets

Ages:

6- to 8-year-olds

Equipment:

Felt	Old mop top (clean and dry)
Glue	Tape
Old clean socks	Scissors
Pipe cleaners	Markers

Prep Time:

5 minutes

Activity:

Using a stash of old socks, have the campers decorate the socks like hand puppets. They can make animals, people, or anything they like. Instruct campers to cut out different shapes in the felt to create eyes, mouths, and ears for their sock puppets. Campers can glue the features onto the toe area of each sock. Pre-cut shapes will help make the designing part run more smoothly. After they are done designing their puppets, divide into smaller groups and have puppet shows. A large sheet placed over a table or the side of a bed will make a stage for the campers to sit behind and hold their puppets above. The counselors might decorate the table while the campers are making their puppets. The counselors can also help with skit ideas.

Variations:

- Recreate a nursery rhyme/fairy tale.
- Re-tell a Bible story.
- Do a newscast of a favorite camp event from the day before.

Balloon Animal Races

Ages:

Any

Equipment:

Lots of long balloons	Scotch tape
Balloon pump, if available	Scissors
Felt	1-inch sections of plastic straws
Construction paper	Ball of string
Glue Stick (do not use hot glue)	

Prep Time:

5 minutes

Activity:

This activity allows any age group to be creative, use their imagination, and build some team spirit. The activity is centered around making flying birds. Campers or cabin groups, working together as a team, create balloon birds using the equipment listed. The culminating event of the activity is a balloon-bird race. To make the bird, campers can either twist and turn the balloons like a clown would do, and/or they can use the balloon for the central body and then create the legs, feet, head, and tail using construction paper and felt. The knotted end of the balloon serves as the tail end of the bird. Cut a one-inch section of a plastic straw and carefully tape it to the top of the bird. The open ends of the straw should be pointing to the front and back of the bird and not obstructed on either end. The group should determine guidelines for participants to follow as they create their birds (e.g., a height, weight, or length maximum) to ensure that each bird has a fair chance in the race. Each bird should be examined to confirm that all birds are equal. The birds can also be judged based on their creativity, color, beauty, or ugliness, etc.

A counselor (and a few campers who finish early) can set the stage for the race. Cut a long section of string for each bird. The strings should be long enough to stretch the length of the race area and should be even. One end of the race area should be higher than the other to give the birds the ability to fly. The birds will begin at the higher end, and with the help of gravity, race to the bottom. If you perceive that the weather is going to clear, a hill outside with two trees is perfect for use as a race area.

Position the birds for the race by putting the high end of the string through the straws taped to each bird and tying the lower end. Do not tie the upper end until the bird can be threaded on the string. Hold onto the bird so that it does not fly yet. Once all birds are on their individual strings and evenly lined up, a counselor will say "Go!" Each participant or team representative, in unison, will use a pair of scissors to cut the knotted end off the balloon. As soon as the cut is made, the birds take flight! Each participant or team can cheer on their own bird. Participants can create new birds and begin the race again. This activity can be as long as the group's enthusiasm lasts.

NOTE: Be aware of possible allergies; this is not a good activity for children who are allergic to latex. Take into consideration children who may be frightened easily by the noise of popping balloons.

Variations:

- Turn the project into an all camp project with cabin group birds.
- Use this to teach a lesson about birds.
- Do the activity with two team members working together.

Funny Faces

Ages:

6-year-olds and up

Equipment:

Large balloons	Glue
Felt	Paint
Markers	½-inch elastic
Construction paper	Large containers to hold water
Plaster of paris strips a paste of newspaper, flour, and water	Optional: egg crates, cardboard, or empty milk bottles
Scissors	

Area:

Covered outdoor area or indoor space
(A place that can be cleaned up easily)

Prep Time:

15 – 30 minutes

Activity:

For this activity you will be making papier mâché masks that can be worn for a play, a costume party, or whatever you choose. To prep for this activity, begin by setting out the large bowls of water and the plaster of paris strips (if you don't have plaster of paris, use strips of newspaper, flour, and water to make a paste). The group can be divided into pairs, with each pair working on one balloon. Each pair will need to blow up a balloon to the size mask they think they will want and then knot the end of the balloon. Next use the plaster of paris strips to cover the balloon. It is important that they try to cover all sections of the balloon and smooth out all bumps and edges. Once the balloon is covered, it should be put in a spot where it can dry overnight. It will take between twelve and twenty-four hours for the plaster to fully dry.

After the plaster is fully dry, each pair can reclaim their balloon. Using a pin, the pair can pop the balloon inside the plaster covering. The plaster should maintain its shape if it has been allowed sufficient time for drying. One partner should carefully cut the papier mâché balloon in half so that there are two equal halves to be used as masks (the younger groups will need help cutting out the masks and making holes for the eyes).

Older participants may want to use the optional items listed above for the nose, eyebrows, lips, and ears of their masks. Cover the facial features of the mask with an additional layer of plaster of paris. Adding plaster of paris to the masks extends this activity into a three-day project. After your additional facial features have had time to dry or your basic mask is dry, you can use paint, markers, felt, and construction paper to give each mask its own character. Remember to cut holes for the eyes and mouth.

To make the mask wearable, fasten a length of one-half-inch elastic to the two vertical sides of the mask. When measuring for the elastic, have the camper hold the mask so that they can see out the eye holes and then place the elastic at the appropriate place. Do not worry about the nose, mouth, and ears lining up, only the eyes.

Variations:

- Make animal masks instead of people masks.
- With the use of cardboard instead of a balloon, you can make any shape you want.
- Write and produce a skit with the masks.

Honey, Do You Love Me?

Ages:
8- to 10-year-olds

Equipment:
None

Prep Time:

None

Activity:

This is a relaxing, slow-paced game, which can start the giggles with any group. The goal of the game is to make someone laugh. Begin by forming a circle with one person in the middle. You need to know two phrases for the game: "Honey do you love me?" and "Honey, I love you, but I just can't smile." The one in the middle ("the asker") must walk up to someone else in the circle and ask the question, "Honey, do you love me?" And the person in the circle must respond, "Honey, I love you, but I just can't smile," without smiling. The "asker" can do anything they want to get the person to laugh except touch them. This rules out all tickling, pinching, etc. Singing, dancing, weird faces, are all acceptable. If the person in the circle does not laugh, the "asker" should move on to another person. However, once someone does smile, they are now the one in the middle, and their spot is taken by the previous "asker." To be fair to everyone, be specific about what constitutes a smile or laugh. It can become very difficult to keep a straight face during this activity, and the group should determine a few game rules, including whether it is okay to laugh after they take their turn in the middle of the circle, whether a half smile puts the player in the middle, etc.

Sneak

Ages:

8- to 11-year-olds

Equipment:

Blindfold

Activity:

Good listening skills are needed for this game. The group stands in a large circle. One camper is blindfolded and stands in one place in the center of the circle. The leader silently points to a camper standing in the circle. That camper will attempt to sneak up to the student in the center of the circle silently, while the rest of the group also remains silent. The object is to get as close as possible and even gently touch the camper in the center. The blindfolded camper has three chances to point directly at the camper sneaking closer. If the camper in the center is successful, the counselor must choose another camper. The blindfolded camper stays in the center until someone touches him or her and the game continues with a new camper in the center.

Keeper of the Fire

Ages:

9- to 12-year-olds

Equipment:

Blindfold

Three sticks

Activity:

The concept of this game is similar to "Sneak." This time, however, the camper blindfolded in the center of the circle is guarding three sticks which symbolize a "fire." The counselor quietly points to one, two, or three campers to sneak up and steal the sticks. All remain silent during this activity. If the blindfolded camper hears a noise, he or she can point to where that noise is coming from. If they point to one of the "sneakers," that camper returns to the circle and a replacement is silently chosen. Play continues until a stick has been stolen. The successful thief becomes the new "keeper of the fire."

Variations:

- Choose one object to place in the middle of the circle, the middle person is not blindfolded and therefore tags instead of points at a camper that gets too close.

- Announce a category to determine who tries to retrieve the sticks (e.g., anyone who has traveled outside their home state, anyone who has been to the beach, anyone who likes to read).

Zooma Zooma

Ages:
10-year-olds and up

Equipment:
None

Prep Time:
None

Activity:
This activity is very similar to the game Concentration, for those of you that remember that game! Begin by having everyone sit in a circle with their legs crossed. Each person in the circle gets a number beginning with the number one. The counselor's number is "zooma zooma." The initial count always begins with "zooma zooma." The count always follows a rhythm of slapping your knees and clapping your hands. The steady rhythm is two knee slaps followed by two hand claps and then repeated over and over again. The speech follows the same rhythm, and you say your number on each knee slap. Then, you say another person's number on each hand clap; for example, if you were the number one and you wanted to call on number three, you would say, "one, one" on the knee slaps and then "three, three" on the hand claps. After you have said this, the player called must respond by saying their number on the next knee slaps and someone else's number on the hand claps. The key is to stay within the rhythm of the game, should you not be paying attention and miss a beat, the game stops, and the players start again. When the game restarts, it always begins with the "zooma zooma" person. Once the group gets better at the game, you can speed up the rhythm.

Printed Bandanas

Ages:
8-year-olds and up

Equipment:
Thin sponges

Scissors

Non-toxic fabric paint

Light-colored bandana for each camper

Fine point permanent marker (Sharpie)

Area:
Cabin space

Prep Time:
5 minutes

Activity:
Bandanas are often popular head gear for many kids. During this activity, each person will have the opportunity to design their own bandana. The prints will be made using sponges that are cut to a particular design. The sponges can be cut in any design the campers decide, be it stars, animal footprints, trees, animals, etc. Have some stencils or previously cut designs the campers can use to trace. Once each person has decided what print(s) they want to use, they need to draw the print onto the sponge using the permanent marker and then cut the sponge. Using the fabric paint, each sponge can be dipped into the paint so that it has a light coat of paint on the sponge's surface. If the layer of paint is too thick, it will turn out thick and gooey on the bandana. Also, be sure to rinse the sponges between color changes. In case the sponge prints aren't clear, have some paint brushes on hand. Also, have a few extra bandanas available in case there are major mistakes. Give all the bandanas at least a few hours to dry before wearing them.

Tin-Bucket Skits

Ages:
8-year-olds and up

Equipment:
(sample list of random cabin supplies)

Bucket	Rubber bands
Clean plunger	Cups
Roll of toilet paper	Sleeping bag
Broom	Book

Prep Time:
5 minutes

Activity:
Begin by gathering as many random items as possible from around the cabin area. The more versatile the items the better. Divide the group into smaller groups of three and four members. Randomly divide the items you have gathered up between the groups. Every group should have the same number of items. Each group has ten minutes to prepare a skit based on the items they have. There is no trading of the items, and it can be about anything they want (within reason). You will want to circulate from group to group in case they are having trouble coming up with ideas or agreeing on a skit. Each skit should be no longer than five minutes. After the skits are prepared, give campers the chance to perform for the cabin in a "stage" area.

Variations:
- Limit the group to one item that every person must use during the skit.
- Join another cabin to do the skits.
- Perform for the director or some specialty staff.
- Have each group use exactly the same items.

Fun with Stories

Ages:
10-year-olds and up

Equipment:
Pencils

Paper

Prep Time:
None

Activity:
For this activity, divide the group into pairs. Each pair will design their own story, but the stories are made up in a special way. Each partner will always write two lines to the story at one time, but they should only be able to see the last line written by their partner while they are writing their two lines. Begin by numbering a piece of paper (one through ten) vertically. Each number will be a line of the story. The first partner will write lines one and two. When they are finished, they will fold over the line so that the next person can only see line two. The next partner writes lines three and four based on what line two reads, folds over lines two and three so that the next person can only read line four, and passes the paper on to his or her partner. This next person then writes lines five and six based on what they read in line four. The paper is then folded over hiding lines four and five. This continues until each pair has written ten lines; the tenth line is the conclusion of the story. When the groups complete their stories, unfold the whole paper and ask the groups to share their stories out loud. They are usually very funny!

Variations:
- Add more lines and the whole group can write one story.
- Create a picture of someone instead by folding over different body parts and identifying who will draw which body part.

Identity Crisis

Ages:
9-year-olds and up

Equipment:
Tape

Paper

Pencils and pens

Prep Time:
5 – 10 minutes

Activity:
Begin with a scrap of paper for each person in the group. On each paper write down the name of someone who the campers would recognize. It can be a movie star, a rock star, a cartoon character, a staff member, etc. Make sure that it is appropriate for the age group. (A nine-year-old may not know who Dolly Parton is, but they will know the cartoon character "Pokemon.") Once there is a different identity for everyone, tape the paper to each person's back where they can't see it. Each camper must figure out their "identity" by asking questions. The activity ends when everyone has figured out what identity they were assigned.

Variations:
- Limit the questions per person, allowing each person to ask one question each time they talk to someone else.
- Limit talking, responses cannot be in speech form only gestures (limit the spelling also).
- Keep all the identities in one category, for example, cartoon characters only.
- Have the group act out there identity at the end of the activity.

Guided Journaling

Ages:

9-year-olds and up

Equipment:

Construction paper

Scissors

Glue

Various markers, pencils, and crayons

Cardboard

Old magazines

Yarn or pipe cleaners

Hole puncher
(a three-hole punch is ideal)

Prep Time:

15 minutes

Activity:

Journaling to some people is boring. Others may not know what to write in a journal or when to write anything in it. This activity offers fun and imaginative ideas to motivate campers to write down their camp experiences. Campers will go home with a colorful journal full of memories that will last a lifetime.

To make the contents and cover of the journal, campers should have a mix of colored construction paper. Start by folding each paper in half with a good crease. Then cut or tear along the middle crease so that there are two pieces of paper for each one original sheet of paper; these will be the pages of the journal. Next, cut two pieces of cardboard, measuring the same size as your journal pages. The cardboard pieces will be the front and back cover of the journal. Cut up images, letters, etc., from old magazines to personalize the journal cover. Once this decorating is finished, use a three-hole puncher to punch three holes in a vertical line on the left side of the cover and on the right side of the back. In the same way, hole punch (left side only) all journal pages, being sure that the holes in the pages match up with those on the cover and backside. After the holes have been punched, match up the cover and back cover with the pages so that all the holes are lined up. Use the string or pipe cleaners to tie the journal together. After assembly, the journal should look like a book.

Once the journal is assembled, each camper can decorate and personalize their journals. You can make journal writing a fun, creative, and interesting project by giving campers topics to write about and some tips on page design. Have campers create places within the pages for "Kodak moments," including their picture, a best friend's picture, a current boyfriend/girlfriend picture, and photos of special camp activities. To make a place for the pictures to slip right into a page, cut small slits into the paper where the corners of a photograph would slide into. Depending on the camp and funds available, it may be possible to convince the director to develop film the next day, so that the pictures can be inserted into the journal before the end of camp. Campers will most likely have plenty of cameras and film with them. Be careful to make sure that all of the campers are included in photographs so no one gets left out. Tell campers to reserve space for addresses and phone numbers of camp friends. Campers can decorate pages listing their favorite things to do and their favorite foods. You can suggest labeling sections in the journal for certain themes, such as the funniest moment at camp, camp friends, favorite activities, and most importantly, remind campers to leave lots of blank pages for writing.

It is important that the counselor set aside some time each day or every other day for journal or reflection time. During these set times, give the campers a subject to write about, whether it is the day's events, the biggest challenge of the day, their biggest accomplishment since they arrived at camp, or what they learned about themselves, etc. Giving campers a subject to reflect on can help spark a stream of consciousness that may lead to other reflections. Reflection allows for learning and allows for better memories of camp. If you know ahead of time the subjects you are going to use, pre-label the pages and let the campers choose which subject to write about during journal time. Be sure not to focus the journals solely on reflection so campers do not lose interest.

Variations:

- Make hand-made paper to use as journal pages.
- Cover the front and back covers with wrapping paper.
- Use Polaroid pictures or the Polaroid Sticky Film for instant pictures.
- Give out pens with the camp logo to each person for future journal entries.
- Tie the pen to the journal using string and some good knots.
- Put nature items in the journal, such as a significant leaf.
- Give each person a camp bumper sticker or sticker to put on their journal to remind them of camp, and this is good advertising for the camp.
- Use silver and gold paint pens on black paper to give it pizzaz!
- Have campers sign each others' books like a memory book.

Camper Squares

Ages:
11-year-olds and up

Equipment:

Masking tape	Paper
Newsprint	Markers

Prep Time:
20 minutes

Activity:
This activity is very similar to the game show "Hollywood Squares" — it is a human game of tic-tac-toe! In order for an "X" or an "O" to get a square they must earn it. Begin by drawing a huge tic-tac-toe board on the floor of the cabin with masking tape. Then place nine of your campers on the board, one in each space. Each space should have a piece of paper that has an "X" on one side and an "O" on the other

side. Next divide the rest of the group into two teams, the "X" team and the "O" team. One counselor should have a list of questions prepared that involve the history of camp, counselors' names, nature facts, and/or anything about camp that the campers may have learned already. To determine the team that goes first, flip a coin. To earn a space on the board, the first team will choose a place to start on the board, and they will need to name the person sitting in that space. The leading counselor/host will ask the chosen camper a question. After the camper has answered it, it is up to the current team to agree or disagree with the answer. If they agree and the camper is right or if they disagree and the camper is wrong, the team gets the space. If they agree and the camper is wrong or if they disagree and the camper is right, the opposing team gets the space. The camper will hold up the appropriate marking for the space. For example, if "X" gets the square, then an "X" will be held up, if "O" gets the square an "O" will be held up. The rules for tic-tac-toe then apply. You must get three "X's" or "O's" in a vertical, horizontal, or diagonal line to win. If there is no winner and the board is full, the team with the most spaces wins. After a round of play, you can mix up the teams or change the campers in the spaces around. Try to keep everyone involved during the game, and play multiple rounds.

Variations:

- Do a bingo sheet instead of tic-tac-toe.
- Make all your questions about nature.
- Use the staff for all the spaces.

Decorative Candle Holders

Ages:

9-year-olds and up

Equipment:

Small glass votive holders   Old paint brushes

Tissue paper   Craft enamel spray

Elmer's glue

Prep Time:

5 minutes

Activity:

This is an easy activity for campers to do that allows them to take something nice home. In small bowls thoroughly mix together a little Elmer's glue and a little water. Then holding the tissue paper around the votive holder, brush the glue mixture right over the tissue paper. The tissue paper can be kept as smooth as each person desires or it can be made bumpy with curves. Each votive holder will be unique to the camper that designed it! Allow several hours to dry and then spray with a craft enamel to seal the coating.

Camp Newspaper

Ages:

11-year-olds and up

Equipment:

Paper	Old magazines
Pencils	Old newspapers
Scissors	Potential to make many copies

Prep Time:

10 minutes

Activity:

This is a great activity to harness the many talents within the cabin group. Inform the campers that they will be developing a newspaper consisting of different elements of their choosing, e.g., comic strips, the news of the day, program activities, menus, or special events, anything that strikes the campers as interesting. Begin by letting the group choose the sections they want to include. This is a good time to look through old magazines and newspapers for ideas. After the campers have chosen the sections, split the group into teams, assigning a section of the newspaper to each team. Remember to include a team that will create the layout for the newspaper. If you have access to a computer, this would be a great advantage. Otherwise, you will need to write everything by hand and cut and paste. You could ask a staff member who is a fast typist to type the articles and print them for the group. Try to limit the newspaper to one page front and back and add pictures if possible. When the whole paper is finished, ask the camp director to photocopy enough copies for every table in the dining hall or for each camper. Depending on how many are copied, they can be posted around camp or given out at the next meal. It may even become a daily activity after the first edition is run.

NOTE: The campers may be really excited about this type of activity. Always remember to edit what is written and keep everything in good taste. Words can be very hurtful when used poorly.

Variations:

- Do comic strips only.
- Have the entire camp pitch in.
- Work with another cabin group.
- Build up anticipation among the rest of campers with a teaser edition at lunchtime.

Head Elephant

Ages:
11-year-olds and up

Equipment:
None

Area:
Cabin area

Prep Time:
None

Activity:

The object of the game is to be the "head elephant." Sitting in a circle, each member of the group picks an animal sign or motion. Usually the person leading the game is the "head elephant," therefore, his or her animal sign is an elephant. It is important for campers to remember their animal signs. The game begins with the head elephant doing his or her sign once and then following it with another camper's animal sign. That camper must now repeat his or her animal sign and follow it with another individual's animal sign. The game continues until someone is not paying attention and breaks the cycle. When that camper breaks the routine, he or she must get up and move to the farthest seat from the head elephant, and everyone else moves up one chair toward the head elephant. When each camper moves to the next seat, he or she must take on the sign of the last individual who sat there. The object of the game is to move up to the head-elephant spot. The only way for a camper to get there is by a camper in front of them in the circle to break the cycle and move to the last seat, and as a result, moving everyone one seat ahead. This activity can be a riot, because it is difficult for each camper to remember his or her own animal sign when it changes so often. Creative animal signs add to the fun.

Variation:

Use numbers instead of animal signs.

BIG Spaces Needed

Cake or Cookie Decorating

Ages:
Any

Equipment:

Pre-baked cakes or cookies	Plastic decorating tips for icing
Non-sharp knife (butter knife)	Parchment triangle
Pre-made icing	Practice board
10-inch or 12-inch pastry bag	Basic color set
Sprinkles/decorative candies	Turntable with stand

Coupler (allows changing of tips without changing bag or use store-bought icing tubes with plastic tips)

Area:
Dining or kitchen area

Prep Time:
Depends on your kitchen staff

Activity:
You can arrange to have a special cake decorating class that decorates cakes or cookies for dessert in the dining hall that night. The class should be conducted by a staff member who is skilled in cake decorating. The equipment list may change or vary depending on the staff member's skill level. Each table in the dining hall should have a cake or set of cookies when the class is finished. The program staff will want to work closely with the kitchen staff to help the class go smoothly.

Variation:
"Play up" the experience with chef's hats, aprons, etc.

Fire Starters

Ages:

8-year-olds and up

Equipment:

Newspaper	Coffee can
Twine	#10 tin can
Crayons to melt for color	Hot plate
Large chunks of dry wax (old candles work, too)	

Area:

Arts and crafts building preferably

Porch area possible

Prep Time:

Enough time for wax to melt — 30 – 60 minutes

Activity:

Everyone knows how difficult it can be to get a fire started in the rain. A wax fire starter almost guarantees that any fire can be lit in the rain. This is a perfect morning activity if the group is cooking outdoors later that evening. One of the most important things to remember when doing this activity is to pay special attention to the hot wax and the hot plate the wax is on. It is very easy to burn the skin when doing this activity.

To begin, fill the #10 tin can with water — about one-fourth to one-half full. Then place the dry wax and crayons in the coffee can. The coffee can should then be placed inside the tin can on the hot plate. Someone should be constantly watching the hot plate. The wax will take about thirty to sixty minutes to melt and will require stirring to help break up the chunks. While the wax is melting, the rest of the group can work on making the base of the fire starters. To make the base, roll together bunches of newspaper. You will need to cut the newspaper so that the base is no more than four inches long. In order to secure the rolled newspaper, tie a piece of twine around the rolled newspaper. You should have at least 6 inches of excess twine after securing the newspaper. This excess twine will then be used to hold onto while dipping. Once the base of the fire starters are made and the wax is melted, it is time to dip. Have the campers form a straight line behind the hot wax can. One at a time, they will each come and holding onto the top of the twine, dip the base of the fire starter into the hot wax for five seconds. After they have dipped the base in, they should go to the back of the line to wait for another turn. Each base should be dipped several times to gain a good amount of wax. The counselors will have to judge when enough wax is on each base. When finished, turn off the hot plate and hang all the fire starters to dry. Now whenever a quick fire is needed, place this fire starter at the base of the fire and it will act like a candle and to help start the fire.

NOTE: Closer and more organized supervision is required for younger ages.

Variations:

- Make drip candles using wicks instead of twine and newspaper.
- Make sand candles.

Radio Program

Ages:

11-year-olds and up

Equipment:

PA system with microphone

CD player

Paper and pencils

Prep Time:

15 minutes

Activity:

This is an excellent opportunity for a group of campers to put on their very own radio program to entertain the rest of camp. Begin by deciding the length of the radio program. The length of the program should be based on the group's enthusiasm and ability to organize the needed program materials. Once a time frame has been decided, start organizing some topics and program material that will be included in the radio show. Programming options include: top ten music hits, commercials, camp news, and radio stories. By dividing the larger group into smaller groups, campers can work on different sections of the radio program. Assign one additional group to strictly work on the production side of the program. Production includes keeping all the sections on time, editing the material that is written, and helping to gather any music or additional technical materials that are needed. This producer group will examine the overall radio program. While organizing the program, begin marketing the radio show to the camp. Let people know when the radio program is scheduled and where they will be able to hear it. It will probably take a few hours to organize the entire radio program, so try not to schedule the air time too early in the day. Once the group is ready, the show should be a hit. You will probably see sides of your campers you have never seen before. Have fun!

Outdoor Play for Mild Rainy Days

Amphibian Bingo Safari

Ages:

6- to 11-year-olds — Make your bingo sheets appropriately.

Equipment:

Laminated bingo sheets and crayons

Area:

A wet marsh-like area, near mud and shallow ponds

Prep Time:

None, if the bingo sheets are pre-made or 1½ hour to make bingo sheets

Activity:

Rain will bring out some wonderful examples of local amphibians. The camp's is location will determine what species can be found. Begin by placing your campers in pairs or trios. Make sure you identify what amphibians are and common places where they can be found. Hand out Bingo sheets with a name of an amphibians listed in each small square. Explain to the group that they are going on an amphibian safari. They will need to try to find as many amphibians as possible. Each time they spot one, they should mark it on their bingo sheet. If they get a full row horizontally, vertically, or diagonally they can yell out "Bingo!" Crayons will write well on laminated bingo sheets. Younger campers may not understand the bingo concept, but they will still enjoy looking for the animals. The nature guide at camp may be able to help staff with the bingo sheets or give ideas on where to go for the amphibian safari. Most amphibians are easier to find in wet areas and on rainy days.

Instructions for Bingo Sheet:

Set up a large square with smaller squares inside of it, similar to a "bingo card." Inside each small square put the names or pictures of different amphibians. When naming the amphibians, specify their color, type, and where it can be found. For example, you might describe a Spring Peeper frog versus the American Toad, in the water or under a rock. The easiest thing to do is to use the same amphibians on each bingo sheet, but change the amphibian names around in the squares on each sheet. If you have the equipment, laminating the sheets will protect them from the weather and allow groups to reuse them several times.

Variations:

- Choose any category of animals.
- Choose things around the cabin or around camp to put on the bingo sheets.
- Follow up the bingo hunt with some discussion at the Nature Center about what amphibians you found and what amphibians they can find when they go home.

Photography

Ages:

A current photography class — 12-year-olds and up

Equipment:

Camera for each person or pair

Film development capabilities

Prep Time:

5 – 20 minutes depending on your setup of materials

Activity:

A rainy day brings out different animals, plants, and scenery. A rainy day is a great opportunity for a photography class to photograph unique things, such as a puddle up-close, a drop of rain on a leaf, or a group of frogs splashing in a puddle. The cloud formations and coloring of the sky can be very unique just after a rainstorm. It may be even be possible to catch a shot of a rainbow. Choose the quality of the cameras based on the age of campers and the quality of photographs desired.

After the pictures are taken is an excellent time to spend indoors developing and learning the art of picture composition. No one will mind being inside learning some basic photography lessons.

Hey Fishy, Fishy

Age:

6- to 9-year-olds

Equipment:

2 ropes for boundaries

Prep Time:

None

Activity:

This is an activity that combines the games "Octopus" and "Mother May I?" into a unique game of tag. Begin by setting up a large rectangular area that is known as the sea. Assign a group of campers to be the "fish." Fish are only safe when they are on the far edges of the sea. Next, ask for two volunteers to begin the game as sharks who are "it." The sharks must stay within the confines of the sea. With all the fish standing on one side of the sea, the sharks say, "Fishy, fishy, come into the sea." The fish respond by saying in unison "How should we come into the sea?" The sharks respond by giving them a method to cross the sea like skipping, hopping, walking, robot style, cowboy style, etc. Then all the fish must cross the sea in this style. If a fish gets tagged by a shark, the fish must stop where they were tagged. At this point, they become seaweed. The seaweed can help the sharks catch all the fish. One game rule to note: the sharks must walk to catch their fish, no running! A counselor may begin as a shark to help the campers think of fun styles of crossing the sea.

NOTE: It is not recommended to use running styles; remember it is raining outside, and the ground is slicker than usual.

Inside Out Projects

Kite Making

Ages:
6-year-olds and up

Equipment:
Tissue paper

Glue

2 thin dowel rods or thin sticks

Needle and thread

Yarn

Area:
Cabin space

Prep Time:
5 minutes

Activity:
The concept behind this activity is to prepare the group for the next sunny day and increase the excitement for the next moment that the rain stops, and the sun shines. What makes this activity so much fun is that the campers can decorate the kites anyway they wish, using easy-to-obtain supplies, and they can even fly their kites backwards. Start the activity by setting the dowel rods at ninety degree angles to each other in a cross pattern. Place the horizontal rod slightly higher than the middle of the vertical rod. You will want to tie the rods together where they meet. Next, lay a large sheet of tissue paper down on the table and spread some glue on one side of the connected dowel rods. Then, lay the glue side down on top of the tissue paper and leave five minutes to dry. Once dry, cut off the excess tissue paper by going from point to point of the rods, forming a diamond shaped kite. Check to be sure the glue has completely dried on the rods before bending the horizontal rod slightly in the

opposite direction of the tissue paper. The kite should have a slightly concaved shape. Use the needle and thread to make a loop near the top of the kite. Where the loop has been made, tie a long length of yarn going out from the tissue paper side. The final step is decorating the kites. Use streamers, feathers, and other light-weight decorations to make each kite unique. When the sun comes out, the kite can be flown with the tissue side facing into the wind, backwards.

Variation:

Think of a "theme" for making kites, like "Soar Above the Crowd" and have campers make the kites to use as decorations (and at-home reminders) of their days at camp.

Catapult

Ages:

11-year-olds and up

Equipment:

(for each group)

2 bicycle tubes	Square of felt
1 plunger	Pipe cleaners
3 water balloons	Ribbon
3 balloons filled with washable, non-toxic paint	Duct tape

Area:

Covered outdoor area for construction

Outside lawn area for launching

Prep Time:

10 minutes

Activity:

Many major sporting events like baseball and basketball games, use a slingshot device to shoot t-shirts and other team give-aways into the stands. The campers will build a similar contraption using the above materials. Divide the group into two teams — preferably no more than ten campers on each team. Each group will receive a set of equipment. Using the equipment given, each group must put together a catapult or slingshot. Once constructed, campers can be given three water balloons to use in order to test their system before using paint balloons. A target to shoot for is easier to identify as opposed to the farthest shot. Each team should be given a time limit to work on their catapults and to test them. An hour to an hour and a half should be sufficient and will encourage groups not to take too long. All practice shots or launches should be done out in the open away from other groups. Make sure that safety is maintained during this activity.

Once all groups have finished their construction, give each group their set of paint balloons. Suggest to the teams that they color code the balloons they plan to shoot from the catapult so they are easier to spot. The paint will help measure where each group's balloon has popped and landed. Plus, when the group is finished with the activity, all the paint can be easily washed away. When the teams are finished, please be sure to pick up all broken balloon pieces.

Variations:

- On a dry day, put chalk circles on a black top to make a large target and just use water balloons.

- Using water balloons only, have your camp director or another staff member be your center target. This is great for a really hot summer day!

Chapter Two

Large Groups/Combination of Two or More Small Groups

(25 – 40+ campers, relatively close in age)

Cabin Fun

Around the Camp in an Afternoon

Ages:
Any

Equipment:
Various board games or indoor camp games

Prep Time:
15 minutes

Activity:
Camps usually have various board games around like Checkers, Risk, and Parcheesi. And, most counselors have a handful of games they can play inside like Concentration, Duck Duck Goose, and many more. Arrange a game that will be played in each cabin. Make sure that a different game can be played in each cabin to add variety. Each cabin group will travel from cabin to cabin, playing different games each time. One staff member should stay at each cabin to run the specified game(s). Also, set a rotation schedule that allows ample time for each game to be played, but not too much time so that campers do not get bored. The counselor running the game should have at least one extra game in their mind that they can use if they have a lot of extra time. A camp bell or whistle can be used to signal each rotation time to keep everyone on schedule.

Counselor-Camper Day

Ages:
Any

Equipment:
None

Prep Time:
Varies by age group

Activity:
Campers elect peers to be the director, nurse, waterfront staff, etc. In each cabin one camper is elected to be the counselor for a period of time. Consider rotating through the day. The "new staff" assumes the role of their elected position (with some guidance). For example, the "new" director for the day may assume their role by making the announcements, and taking on whatever the director does that day. Nurse for the day, assists the real nurse all day. The real counselors play the roles of the campers who are taking their place. The waterfront staff assists the real waterfront staff for the day. This can be fun as campers see the counselors act like campers and vice versa. Be sure to remind the staff that they are still responsible for their group's activities. They may assist their new counselor in any way needed. Also remind the staff not to go overboard in their camper roles.

Specialized Activities

Ages:
Any

Equipment:
Depends on activity

Prep Time:
Depends on activity

Activity:
Find out the special talents of your staff and conduct special activities not usually offered in good weather. There may be a staff member who is a black belt in Karate, one who can teach juggling, and one who is skilled at teaching aerobics. There are lots of special talents that the staff will have. Make sure the camp is utilizing those talents.

Fashion Show

Ages:
10-year-olds and up

Equipment:

Blankets	String
Sheets	Paper and pencil
Masking tape	

Prep Time:
5 minutes

Activity:
This is a great activity for the campers to show their creative side and fashion sense. Join in with several other cabin groups and tell them that each cabin will be putting on a summer fashion show of the latest camp trends. The fashion show will take place in each of the cabins that are represented. Each cabin is assigned a specific

fashion category such as beachwear, evening wear, sportswear, or whatever other categories you can dream up. Be aware of giving the girls the beachwear category, this may not be appropriate. Also set a time limit for each cabin fashion show. After the initial concept has been explained, each cabin should have a designated time to decorate and setup a stage or runway, decide on the fashions to be shown, and designate each person's role. Blankets, sheets, and whatever else is around can be used for stage setup, decorations, or fashions. The designated roles should include an announcer to talk about each style and designer; the "models;" and a pre-show entertainer. The pre-show entertainer is especially important because as the large group travels from cabin to cabin, the host cabin will need time to get ready upon arrival at their own cabin. He or she will keep the large group busy as things are being prepared backstage.

This activity will take up an entire morning, afternoon, or day if the groups are especially creative. The boys may not be genuinely excited at the first thought of a fashion show, but given the correct male vision and direction, they will be just as interested as the girls.

Variation:

Suggest international flavor and décor for the cabins.

BIG Spaces Needed

Rain

Ages:
Any

Equipment:
None

Prep Time:
None

Activity:
This is a wonderful quiet-time activity that can be very calming for a rambunctious cabin group. This activity simulates the sound of a rain storm. The activity is more effective during a soft rain, but is not necessarily advised during the louder thundershowers — unless the cabin blocks out a fair amount of noise. Begin with everyone seated in a circle quietly. Explain that a counselor will be walking around the circle doing a motion like clapping or snapping fingers. It is important that the campers don't start doing the motion the counselor is doing until he or she is in front of the camper. The campers need to continue doing the previous motion until the counselor is again in front of them. It will be similar to a wave of sound. Watch the campers as the counselor goes around and stop if further explanation is needed or do a practice round. Also, tell the campers that in order for this to work they must remain quiet during this activity.

Once the counselor is ready to begin, they will do one motion for the entire circle before starting the next motion. The order of the motions is as follows:

1. Sliding palms together (drizzle),
2. Snapping fingers (constant rain),

3. Slapping legs (pouring rain),

4 stomping feet (thunder),

5. Slapping legs,

6. Snapping fingers,

7. Sliding palms,

8. Stopping the motion while walking around the circle.

When the activity is finished, it should have simulated the same sound as a rainstorm from start to finish. The sounds should be made in a wave. Ask the campers if they can identify what they just heard and ask them name the sound.

Variations:

- Have a camper help the counselor go around the circle.
- If you are knowledgeable, you can talk about how rain is formed and different types of storms.

Indoor Softball

Ages:

8-year-olds and up

Equipment:

Beach ball or large balloon (have extra balloons on hand)

Foam noodle

Bases

Butterfly net or large bucket

Prep Time:

5 minutes

Activity:

This is a new way of playing softball, where the main elements of softball have been given a small twist. First, the usual hard softball is replaced with a beach ball or large balloon. Second, the usual bat is replaced with a foam noodle, use this in any shape chosen. Third, the catchers mitt is replaced with a bucket or large butterfly net. Finally, when running the bases, the runners must hop on one foot or go wheelbarrow style or anything you choose. Make sure the floor is dry when playing this game! The rest of the rules of normal softball/ baseball apply. Cabin groups can be placed against each other or if the cabin group is large enough, create two teams from within the group. Feel free to add more twists to the game, but try not to make it too complicated.

Sing Down

Ages:

9- to 11-year-olds

Equipment:

Paper or chalkboard to keep score and list team names.

Piece of paper and pencil for each team.

Prep Time:

5 minutes

Activity:

The prep time for this activity begins with organizing a list of words to use as themes. Then, when the groups arrive, divide the large group into teams (cabins or otherwise divided). If a counselor remains with each team, the campers will be more enthusiastic about the activity. Next explain to the group that each team's objective is to come up with as many songs that have a specific word like "love" in it. The entire team must be able to sing at least thirty seconds of each song. The more songs they can come up with the better.

When everyone is ready to start the first round, call out the first word. Give each team three to five minutes to prepare a list of songs that fit into that category. After the time is up, call out "pencils down" and point to a team that will start. At this time, the team must begin to sing part of a song that contains the chosen word.

Next, another team is chosen and they must do the same. The game continues until one team cannot sing a song or they repeat a song. If this happens, that team is eliminated and the rest of the groups continue until there is only one team left. (NOTE: The last team must have one song with which to finish the game.)

After there is one team left, assign that team a designated number of points and give points to second and third place also. After a winner is declared, a new category can be announced and the game can begin again.

Sample Theme List:

Dog (or just animals)	Blue
Yellow	Rainbow
Red	Moon
Sun (or sunshine)	Star

Dutch Auction

Ages:

Any

Equipment:

Chalk	Items list
Easel	Panel of judges
Blackboard	

Area:

Indoor or outdoor space

Activity:

During this activity the campers will have the opportunity to be resourceful and imaginative. Before the activity begins each camper should be asked to collect ten to twelve personal items from their cabin and return with these items in a bag. Once they return, the campers should be split into smaller groups of a minimum of twelve campers. During the item collection period the activity leader should either review the sample list below or organize a new list of items to use. Once the activity begins, the leader will read off the items one at a time. As each item is read the small groups have a few minutes to find or create that item within the personal items they have brought with them. Once they have found it or created it, one representative should come to the front of the room so that the leader can approve the item and give points. If there are additional staff available, they can be a "panel of experts" who approve the items presented, awarding a thumbs up, thumbs down, or thumb in the middle (various points for each thumb position). If a small group should send more than one representative, the activity leader may deduct a point(s) from that group. Point deductions will help prevent any mass havoc.

Sample Items List for Dutch Auction:

Poster	Digital watch
Handkerchief	Flowered tennis shoes
Purple button	Gloves
Notre Dame	Poncho
IU drinking cup	Green eyes
Electric toothbrush	Light bulb
Flip-flops	Hair part (left side)
A good joke	Pair of long johns
Funny or scary face	Camera
Calendar	Green pants
Shampoo	Soda can
Relative in audience	Stand on head for 5 seconds
Shoe with an eyelet	Hole in pocket
Missing lower tooth	Comb
Inside out	Blue toothbrush
Boxer shorts	Dial soap
Toothbrush	PJs with animals

Chair Tag

Ages:
9-year-olds and up

Equipment:
Enough chairs for each person to have one

Prep Time:
5 minutes

Activity:
As the title denotes, this is a form of tag and is usually done inside. Begin by arranging all the chairs in a circle. The circle should be tight enough for each chair to be in contact with the chair next to it, since the campers will be sliding from chair to chair and it is easy to fall between chairs.

Begin with everyone seated, then one person must stand up and be in the middle. The goal of the person in the middle is to sit in the empty chair. The goal of everyone else is to keep that person from sitting in the empty chair. The way to prevent the person in the middle from sitting is for the person to the left of the empty chair to slide into it. As they slide into the empty chair, their chair becomes empty until the next person slides into it. Therefore, the placement of the empty chair will move around the circle as the sliding begins. Start off slowly to see how it works. The faster people slide the harder it is for the person in the middle to find the empty chair and sit in it and the more fun it becomes. You will typically find that some laps will be sat on in mistake. If the middle person does find a seat, the person to the left of them is now in the middle and a new empty seat is created.

This game can be lots of fun! It is a great icebreaker to get the laughs rolling and when used with groups of twenty or more is just great to watch. Be careful that the floor is not wet or slippery (remember that wet shoes make wet floors!) and watch for people sliding out of chairs or chairs sliding out of place. These are both very real possibilities when you get going fast.

Variation:

The person in the middle can call "reverse" at any time, reversing the direction of the sliding.

Pictionary/Charades

Ages:
10-year-olds and up

Equipment:
Markers

Newsprint/chalkboard

Masking tape

Prep Time:
10 minutes

Activity:
Most people have played Pictionary and Charades at some time. This activity combines the two games into one. Begin by making a list of categories like the following: movies, television, music, camp history, counselors, etc. Then under these categories brainstorm approximately five titles, words, or phrases that fit within each category. Divide the large group into two or three teams. Each team should also have a stack of newsprint taped to the wall and markers for drawing. During each round, each team will have the same category, phrase, or sentence. Start each round by giving the team volunteers the category and phrase and then choose a method (Pictionary or Charades) for the team volunteers to use to help their team members guess the phrase or sentence. After each group has begun, the counselor can change the method of communication the team volunteer is using at any time by shouting "switch." The team volunteers are then obligated to change their form of communication from Pictionary to Charades or vice versa. Keep the round going until one team guesses correctly. Play as many rounds as desired and keep points for each round. Most

importantly, try to keep everyone involved by changing team volunteers for each round.

Variations:

- Make wheel that spins to pick the category each time.
- Have them pick three words to use and use only those three words and motions to describe the given topic.

Evening Program Design

Ages:

12-year-olds and up

Equipment:

This will depend on the group

Prep Time:

10 minutes

Activity:

Give the older campers a fun lesson in decision making and creativity by allowing them to design an evening program for the younger campers. Offer a framework around the evening such as the time, the equipment available, the ages of the campers, location, and previous programs. Work with the group to help them start brainstorming program ideas. The counselors will need to help facilitate the discussion to make sure everyone participates and stays focused. After the group has the basic theme, they will need to determine the details of the evening including the roles of each person, the timing of activities, equipment needed, and possibly even a snack to distribute. Try to let the campers take ownership for the evening, they will be excited about the responsibility.

Variation:

Use the same concept to plan an all-camp activity.

Highlighter Party

Ages:
11-year-olds and up

Equipment:
1 highlighter marker for each camper

Black lightbulb(s)

Old, dark-colored sheets

Prep Time:
Depends on area you choose to use

Equipment:

This is a party or dance like any other party at camp; however, the unique decor keeps this party from ever being considered boring. The decorative difference is the use of highlighters and sheets. To decorate the party area, hang dark-colored sheets around the room. Then, change a few of the lightbulbs to black light. The black lights will make light-colored items glow in the dark. During the party, the campers can write on the sheets with the highlighters they bring with them. Remind campers that the highlighters cannot be erased and to write in good taste. Inform campers it would be inappropriate to write with the highlighters on another person.

Variation:

This can be used as a closing activity for a cabin group, where they write on shirts for each other and then use a black light to see the inscribed notes.

Dinner and Dancing

Ages:
11-year-olds and up

Equipment:
Stereo

Candles

Decorations

Prep Time:

1 – 2 hours

Activity:

After a day of walking in the rain and getting muddy, the older campers will look forward to taking showers and looking their best. The camp can arrange for this group to have a night of dinner and dancing. Begin by bringing some staff together to decorate the dining hall and put together the music. It should be possible to collect enough CDs from staff and campers to put together an array of music that fits the age group. A particular staff member with disc jockey talents might be willing to volunteer for the evening. Arrange a later dinner than the rest of camp and ask the cooks to prepare a nice meal. Depending on what the campers bring to wear at camp, you can recommend that they dress up. During dinner, let them sit anywhere they want, instead of by cabin, or make seating cards to mix the groups up. After dinner, the dancing can begin. Be sure to leave some drinks and snacks out to quench their thirst and appetites.

Block off the disc jockey area or problems may arise with the campers badgering the DJ with requests and ruining CDs and equipment accidentally. Keep a close eye on the campers, make sure everyone stays inside, and that enough staff are monitoring the outside. Depending on the age, a few campers may be too close together. Consider putting some boundaries or restrictions in place before the music starts. Make sure the staff are aware of appropriate camper behaviors.

All the campers should be very excited at the thought of getting a night to relax and mix with each other. They will definitely look forward to hot showers and a good meal.

Outdoor Play for Mild Rainy Days

Alpha Wolf

Ages:

10-year-olds and up

Equipment:

Long piece of rope or webbing

Emergency flashlight

Prep Time:

10 minutes

Activity:

This is a nighttime activity that simulates the communication of wolves and behavior of wolf pack travel. It is also an alternate way of playing the hide-and-seek. To begin with, the staff should be comfortable with traveling in the dark and the layout of the camp property that will be used. This activity should be played with multiple cabin groups; each cabin represents a pack of wolves. Each head cabin staff should have the equipment listed above.

Inform the large group that each cabin group, i.e., wolf pack, will be trying to locate the Alpha Wolf. In order to find the Alpha Wolf, each pack will have to work together. Working together will involve producing a wolf pack howl, communicating with each other as to how and in what direction they will be traveling, and physically staying together at all times. The wolf pack howl is the key to finding the Alpha Wolf. As the wolf pack howls together, the Alpha Wolf will decide if he likes your howl. If he does he will respond with his howl. All groups will be able to distinguish the Alpha Wolf howl because it is the only singular wolf howl. Then by the sound of the Alpha Wolf, the group can decide which direction to travel.

Before the activity begins, there are a few things that must be covered. First, because they are wolves, once the activity begins no spoken language will be allowed. Therefore each wolf pack will need to decide on a means of communication, using just wolf sounds or other nonverbal cues (clapping, stamping, etc.). Each pack must have a reasonable amount of time to decide how they will communicate with each other once the activity begins. Important points of communication will be "go," "stop," "right," "howl," and other directional words. Each group must remain within the boundaries at all times, and the Alpha Wolf will only travel within the boundaries. Inform each pack that they must stay together at all times. Each pack should have a rope for everyone to hold on to if they wish. The pack will need to travel at the pace of the slowest wolf and keep in mind environmental factors like slick grass. Next, there are no flashlights allowed. The only flashlights will be those that the head counselor has for emergency purposes. The activity will be played in the dark!

Finally, once the group locates the Alpha Wolf, they should sit down next to him and stay quiet until the rest of the groups find him. It is important not to give away the Alpha Wolf's position when the group finds him. As a last safety tip, make sure all the groups know where a central person is located in case they have any unforeseen trouble. All groups should return to the central starting location if they have not found the Alpha Wolf within a set time limit.

Guidelines for the Alpha Wolf:

The Alpha Wolf should have a strong howl that is loud enough to carry throughout the boundaries. The Alpha Wolf should also wear dark-colored clothing so as not to be seen easily. He also has the ability to travel for the first half of the activity time. He does not have to stay in one spot or else the game would end rather quickly. After the first half he should remain in one hidden location so that groups can stay with him upon finding him. The Alpha Wolf also does not have to respond to all wolf pack howls, only the ones he likes. He should never respond to a singular howl, only pack howls. Finally, the Alpha Wolf should return to the starting point after the time limit has ended.

After everyone is clear on all the directions and safety precautions, the Alpha Wolf should be given a five- to-ten-minute head start to begin hiding. This can take place while the directions are being given or while the groups are figuring out their means of communication. Then the activity continues as read above with each wolf pack looking for the Alpha Wolf. Once the game ends and everyone has returned to a central meeting place, be sure that each camper is accounted for.

Variation:

This can be used to teach campers about wolves' behaviors. The activity reflects how wolves move in packs and how there is always one Alpha Wolf in a pack. There is an old recording called *The Language and Music of Wolves* which tells the stories of wolves and their behaviors. Alpha Wolf is a great demonstration of wolf behavior and can easily be used to reflect on the actual ways of wolves.

Inside Out Projects

Scavenger Hunt

Ages:
Any

Equipment:
Items list (make the item list appropriate to age group)

Prep Time:
5 minutes

Activity:
This can be done by blending cabin groups, single cabin groups split into teams, or as just one group. It is easier to keep everyone involved when the teams are smaller in size. Put together a list of items that each group needs to find. The items can include things found in nature such as a frog, a salamander, or a mushroom. They may also include a pink toothbrush, a mirror, or a size thirteen shoe. If it is approved by other camp staff, add items like a whistle from the lifeguard or the director's middle name or a glue stick from the arts-and-crafts instructor. The game is even more interesting when campers are challenged with thought-provoking riddles; for example, you could ask the campers to search for a picture of Abraham Lincoln (a penny or a $5 bill), or a thermometer that reads 100 degrees (can be drawn or can be heated to exactly 100 degrees). There are a variety of things that can be put on the scavenger hunt list. Be creative and don't lose the list. It may be possible to use it for the next session.

When sending camper groups out to find items on the list, make sure that a staff member is present with each group. The ratios of staff to camper depend on the age group. The counselor may consider going to different sections of camp where they are able to keep everyone in eye sight but allow the groups to work more independently. Also, set boundaries and allow no one outside of the boundaries.

You may set a time limit for the activity to increase enthusiasm for finding all the items.

Chapter Three

All-Camp/All Ages

Cabin Fun

Ghost Stories

Ages:
Any

Equipment:
Pen and paper

Prep Time:
None

Activity:

If the rain seems to be nonstop and it looks like the evening activity will have to be inside, this is a great activity that each group can do during the daytime and then all groups can do later that night. Beginning at the start of the day, assign each group to come up with a three- to five-minute ghost story, that will be read later that evening for the whole camp. Each group with the help of their counselors, has the whole day to plan the scariest or grossest ghost story they can come up with. They should also practice reading it before meeting with the whole group. If the groups want to come up with actions or pictures, let them. Remind them that this is not a contest, but a chance to be creative.

Later that night after dinner, instruct each group to meet in a specified area with their stories. When the groups arrive, explain that they will be traveling to each cabin in a specific order. As they arrive at each location, it is the specific cabins's turn to tell their story. The groups can be encouraged to read the story by the light of a single flashlight to really keep the mood going. Once the evening begins, be aware that some groups will tell very real and frightening stories. Make sure the staff is prepared for the possible results of scary stories. There may be lights on that evening all over camp!

Finally, try to remind campers when the evening is over that all the stories were fictional and no pranks are allowed. Otherwise, it may be a long night!

NOTE: Be aware of the audiences that will be hearing the stories, including all age groups and possible religious beliefs.

Indoor Carnival

Ages:

Any

Equipment:

Depends on activities chosen

Prep Time:

25 minutes

Activity:

Many camps have done outdoor carnivals. This is an opportunity to forget about the rain and only change your plans slightly. In this all-camp activity, the campers will be traveling from cabin to cabin for different games and shows. Many of the same games can be played as they are seen at a carnival, for example, knocking down pins — use a soft ball and empty milk cartons so that nothing can be damaged in the cabin. A haunted house can easily be designed in a cabin or a comedy act can fill any cabin with laughter. As an outdoor station, set up two lines about twenty feet apart and put a bucket at each line One bucket should be full of water (with sponges) and one empty. Then set up a relay where the group has to try to fill the empty bucket using the soaked sponged, just remember no running and to keep plenty of dry towels on hand for the end of the activity. In another cabin the campers can tell Native American stories or ghost stories. All the campers will have the opportunity to visit each cabin on their rounds and they will enjoy seeing other campers homes as well as the different activities at each station.

Decide early on which activities will be in the cabins and then each cabin group can decorate accordingly. They can also do a super cleaning job to prepare for everyone's entrance. Remind the campers to put away anything that is valuable or could get broken or that they wouldn't want anyone else to see. Plus, remind everyone not to invade another person's privacy when entering different cabins. Finally, remind campers to try not to track in mud or leaves into others cabins, especially after everyone has worked hard to clean them earlier in the day!

Clue

Ages:
Any

Equipment:
Depends on the characters

Prep Time:
60 – 90 minutes

Activity:
Most people have played the board game "Clue." This is a dramatized version. Begin by creating a fictional murder case. Decide who was murdered, the tool, or weapon used in the murder, the place the body was found, the time it occurred, and who found the body. Next organize a list of characters that could be potential suspects — five to ten suspects is more than enough. They should each have their own character background and should be linked somehow as a possible suspect to the murder. The characters should have names and a general description. They can be the actual camp staff or can be fictional such as a wrestler, sports player, or musician. The activity is more fun if a broad range of characters are chosen. The staff will be portraying these characters. Next, after you have the characters and the fictional murder organized, give each character a fact or two that they have to answer correctly, when asked. Between all the characters, they should have the facts necessary to solve the mystery.

After this preparation has been done, assign the characters a place around camp to be stationed until the end of the activity. Now, once the campers arrive for the activity, have them all sit down and build up the story of the murder. Let them know that it is up to them to help the police solve the crime. Each group should have a map which tells them where all the characters are stationed and a designated place to start. It is possible to give each group a designated time frame for each station, if the camp chooses. At each station the group has to ask the different suspects questions to solve the case. As mentioned above, the characters will have one or two facts that they have to answer correctly; therefore, if the group asks the right question, they will be able to gather all the information they need to solve the crime.

If the staff can play their roles well, the campers will really enjoy the activity and enjoy going to talking to different suspects. Try not to make it too complicated the first time this activity is tried. Also, refer to the board game for some other helpful hints.

BIG Spaces Needed

Haunted House

Ages:
Any

Equipment:
Construction paper, scissors, tape, glue, creepy music, cotton balls, various other items handy that may be requested.

Prep Time:
All-day event for the campers plus 15 minutes to schedule and prepare equipment

Activity:
On a really wet day, when campers may not have much interest in spending time in the great outdoors, turn your large, indoor space into a haunted house. With the proper preparation and creative instincts, this can be turned into an all-day activity. The house itself maybe the dining hall or large indoor recreation space or barn. Give the older campers time during the day to make decorations for the haunted house and design haunted house activities. Give them as much creative freedom, as possible. A common example of an activity is the use of peeled grapes as eyeballs. When campers can't see the grapes, they can feel like eyeballs. They also might design a series of dark or partially lit tunnels and places for your younger campers to go through. Be sure to also give them enough time to design costumes for the evening. The whole camp can come dressed for the occasion. There can even be a costume judging contest for all ages and different categories. Be sure that the older groups can coordinate some of the events and decorations within the haunted house. The younger campers throughout the day can put their costumes together and maybe decorate jack-o-lanterns or table centerpieces. Finally, be careful that the pranks or activities inside the house are not going to leave nightmares behind!

NOTE: Consider any religious beliefs that campers may have plus age-appropriate activities.

Variations:

- Consider a Halloween dance.
- Consider going from haunted cabin to haunted cabin where there is something different in each cabin.
- You can make it any holiday or theme as long as you don't discriminate any campers.

Talent Show

Ages:

Any

Equipment:

Possibly a CD player/tape player, sheets, rope, towels, masking tape, things that are handy

Area:

Large indoor space to seat the whole camp

Prep Time:

General staff-none; campers — most of the day; specialist staff and directors — half a day

Activity:

This is most appropriate for those days when the forecast says it is going to pour into the night and the rain just isn't going to be letting up. Announce to the camp that a camp-wide talent show will be held in the evening. There should be a talent act from each cabin and prizes given out in various categories. Each act should be no longer than three-to-five minutes. Each cabin has the day to prepare for the show. Give each group a set rehearsal time in the stage area during the day. It is unimaginable that each cabin will spend the entire day working on their acts, but it will take up at least a few hours of daytime activity and will be a great evening activity that keeps the campers interest and keeps them dry. The acts should vary from some truly talented groups to just some funny and bone-tickling acts. Open it up to the use of recorded music and there will be a few teenagers doing some lip-syncing to the latest bands.

During the course of the day, ask your specialist staff or any staff that doesn't have program to ready the stage area. Ask them to be creative with supplies that are laying around, towels, sheets, rope, etc. If there are no available extra staff, cabins can be assigned to work on the stage throughout the course of the day. This will take some coordination on the director's part.

Once the show is ready to begin, be sure to have a good MC or host. It will be important to get the crowd motivated and keep them interested while acts get ready. Don't forget the panel of judges either. They will be the ones deciding the winners. Be sure there are plenty of prize winning categories, everyone should win something. It is never fun to lose. Categories can include: the cutest, the best vocalist, the funniest, etc. A talent show can last as long as the camp wants or it can be a short evening. That will be up to the hosts and judges and the size of the large group.

Variations:

- Do a spin-off of MTV's "Say What? Karaoke."
- There is always the "Gong Show."
- Show the movie "Grease 2" — a talent show movie.

Indoor Olympics

Ages:

Any

Equipment:

Depends on the events chosen

Prep Time:

1 hour

Activity:

The camp may already hold an Olympics day at your camp, but indoor Olympics can be just as much fun. In an indoor Olympics everything should be slower and softer. Instead of running, walk. Instead of boating on the lake, use "dolleys" or "scooters" and paddle across the floor. Instead of soccer outside, play crab soccer inside with a balloon. Instead of shot put with a heavy item, use paper plates. There are a variety of different events that can be done.

When the day is set up there may be age-group events or teams mixed up with different age groups. When the points are handed out to the respective winners, use high numbers like 5,000 points for first place or 2,000 points for first place. The higher the points, the more exciting things can become. Finally, have Olympic prizes for the winners and a snack for everyone.

Suggested events:

Shot put with paper plates	Biggest puddle splash (outside)
Crab soccer with a balloon	Best dance routine
Javelin throw using straws	Egg toss or egg relay race
Canoeing on "scooters"	Paper airplane tosses
Wheelbarrow races	Swim contests (if it's a warm rain)
Walking sprints	Three-legged walking races
Long stride instead of jump	Jump rope
Hockey using straws and Ping Pong® balls	

Float Making

Ages:
Any

Equipment:

Canoes/kayaks

Lots of boxes

Crepe paper

Paper

Markers and crayons

Scissors

Tape

Prep Time:
10 minutes

Activity:

The activity will be reminiscent of a holiday parade with floats decorated in various themes. Each group will have the use of one boat, the younger campers may have smaller boats. Each group can then decorate their boat to look like a parade float. It can be suggested that each group relates their float to the theme of the week or they can choose anything they want. After each group has finished decorating, judge all the floats and reward groups for winning a certain category. If multiple categories are used, everyone can win a prize. Remind the campers not to use glue on the boats and possibly no tape directly on the side of the boat.

Variations:

- Put the boats on scooters and they will roll across the floor.
- If it stops raining, put the boats in the water with a "Float King or Queen."

One-Utensil Meal

Ages:

Any

Equipment:

All different eating utensils (according to age)

An empty container for each table

Prep Time:

5 minutes

Activity:

Be creative with one of your meals during the day. Pick a meal where the camp would usually use silverware. Before the group arrives, take empty containers and fill them with different types of eating utensils. Then as each group sits at their table to eat, they can reach into the container and choose a utensil to use. They then need to use that utensil only for the rest of the meal. Beware, it may take longer to finish this meal than usual.

Variation:

Tell everyone, there's been a shipwreck or massive storm, and these were the only utensils they could save.

Outdoor Play for Mild Rainy Days

Counselor Hunt

Ages:
Any

Equipment:
Extra flashlights (may not need, but good to have handy)

Prep Time:
30 minutes

Activity:
This activity can be done at any time during the day, but makes an especially nice evening activity because darkness will make for better camouflaging. The first thing that needs to be determined is the number of groups there will be by deciding how to split the campers into teams. The teams can be cabin groups or can be mixed ages. Determine the number of counselors that need to remain with the group (this will vary per age group — check the ACA Standards guide to determine the ratios needed). After the counselors that will remain with the groups stand aside, determine how many staff members are remaining. Try to have at least the same number of staff members hide as the number of teams searching. Next give the hiding counselors some guidelines about hiding. These guidelines should include the use of high areas (trees, roofs, etc.), the boundaries, time limit, the home base, and instructions for when they are caught.

Once the counselors understand their limits, go ahead and announce to the campers that there is going to be a counselor hunt. Let them take a good look at who they will be hunting and how many counselors will be out there. After this, go ahead and let the counselors hide, will be out there. After this, go ahead and let the counselors hide, being sure that no one will be able to see their hiding places as they take off. While the staff get a head start on hiding, take the time to explain all of the rules. These rules should include the boundaries of the game, what to do when a staff member is found (sign a paper or bring the counselor back), staying as a group the whole time (maybe penalties for whenever the group splits), use of flashlights (if necessary), buildings that are off limits, no tree climbing, time limits, activity leader's location throughout the game for emergencies, and other safety guidelines you think are necessary. Keep in mind that it will be slick outside, so running is not a good idea. Once the campers understand all the rules, give them a few extra minutes to plan as a team what they will do. This will continue to give the counselors extra hiding time. After a few minutes, release all the teams at one time and make sure the activity leader stays in one central area to tend to any emergencies or questions that may arise during the course of the hunt.

Variations:

- Give out different points to the different staff members, therefore, one staff member caught maybe worth more than another.

- Add that the group must stay linked to each other the entire time.

- Assign certain teams to find certain staff, this may help with the different ages of your teams.

- Have each group find the counselors in a specific order.

Inside Out Projects

Guess Who?

Ages:
Any

Equipment:
Sheets

Clothing

Clown makeup, if available

Paper and markers

Prep Time:
Each group will be different

Activity:
Let each cabin group know that for the next meal, they will have the opportunity to dress up their counselor. They need to choose a cartoon character or comic book character to make their counselor look like. They can use whatever resources they have available in their cabins and the camp may provide some clown makeup or paper and markers to help. At the next meal, other cabin groups will have the opportunity to guess who the counselor is supposed to be. Prizes can be given out to the most similar resemblance, the best dressed, the funniest, etc. Make sure that your counselors are willing to go along with this!

Variation:
- Widen your categories of characters, for example, movie stars, singers, etc.

Additional Sources for Rainy Day Projects

Craft Fun with Sondra by Sondra Clark and Silvana Clark

Mud Pies Activity Book Recipes for Invention by Nancy Blakey

175 East-to-Do Everyday Crafts by Sharon Dunn Umnik

Klutz Kids Travel Book by Klutz Press

Stop the Watch by Klutz Press

Multicultural Cooking by Lorraine Barbarash

Stories for the Campfire by Bob Hanson and Bill Roemmich

8820